McDougal Littell

Character
Education

McDougal Littell
A HOUGHTON MIFFLIN COMPANY
Evanston, Illinois • Boston • Dallas

Acknowledgments

Jacques Benninga is a professor at California State University at Fresno in the Curriculum and Instruction department. He teaches classes in Educational Psychology and Early Education and is the director of the Bonner Center for Character Education and Citizenship at Fresno. Dr. Benninga has studied and researched issues related to the moral development and character education of children. Dr Benninga edited the book, Moral, Character and Civic Education in the Elementary School (Teachers College press, 1991) and has published widely in the area of character education.

The Bonner Center for Character Education and Citizenship was formed in 1997 to promote character education in the Central Valley of California. It sponsors nationally recognized speakers, forums or character education and professional ethics materials, books and professional resources for review, and coordinates a variety of character award programs.

Printed in the United States of America.

ISBN-13: 978-0-618-53023-6   ISBN-10: 0-618-53023-1

4 5 6 7 8 9 - CKI - 10 09 08 07 06

Character Education

Table of Contents

Responsibility

Trustworthiness

Character Education

by Jacques S. Benninga, Ph.D.
Director, Bonner Center for Character Education and Citizenship
California State University, Fresno

Although character education is rather a new phenomenon, re-introduced in the 1990s and gaining emphasis through the U.S. Department of Education's *No Child Left Behind* legislation, it has always been at the core of the American public school curriculum. The term *character education* refers to the duty of the older generation to form the character of the young. Thus the purpose of schooling is to teach the next generation both the skills related to academic subjects as well as the skills needed by productive, contributing members of our pluralistic democratic society.

Examples of character education abound in our nation's history. George Washington kept a notebook containing, in his own handwriting, 110 *Rules of Civility in Conversation Amongst Men*. Included in these rules were "Show not yourself glad at the misfortune of another, although he were your enemy," and "Associate yourself with men of good quality if you esteem your own reputation, for it is better to be alone than in bad company." Throughout his life, Washington attempted to live by these rules. Indeed, many of our nation's founders advocated personal rules focused on attributes such as diligence, a strong work ethic, a positive attitude and perseverance, as well as moral habits such as respect for others, civility, and tolerance.

These same lessons also influence the lives of modern heroes. For example, James B. Stockdale, a U.S. Navy pilot shot down over Vietnam in 1965, assumed the leadership of the inmates at the prisoner-of-war camp where he was held. His guidance and example helped his fellow prisoners survive years of mistreatment and torture. He was awarded the Congressional Medal of Honor for his bravery. To survive his imprisonment, Stockdale relied on the lessons he learned from the works of ancient Stoic philosophers. Nancy Sherman, a philosophy professor at Georgetown University, writes that Stockdale cultivated "the inner resources and virtues that allow for a measure of control in the face of strong temptation and hard losses."

The lessons of history and philosophy have been supplemented by research on how children face challenging situations. William Damon of Stanford University, author of *Greater Expectations* (1996), describes research that shows children thrive on accomplishment, not on empty self-esteem messages. Reasonable pressures related to worthwhile activities, including demanding homework, do not overburden them. On the whole, Damon states, children are tough and resilient and are motivated to learn through both extrinsic inducements (e.g., high expectations, rewards, pressure, encouragement, grades, etc.) and intrinsic motivations. They need the guidance that can best be provided by able, caring, concerned adults. And Daniel Goleman, author of *Emotional Intelligence* (1995), documents the effects of positive and counter-productive child-rearing practices that result in either positive or anti-social behaviors. Many of these practices relate to teaching. Such at-risk behaviors as impulsiveness and belligerency, stubbornness and indecisiveness, overreaction to irritation, and inability to put off gratification are learned, and interfere with social and educational success, with what Goleman calls "mental clarity." Other dispositions, equally learned, are much more conducive to optimism and full maturity. These include a strong cultural work ethic, temperance, the ability to cope with frustrations, optimism, and empathy. The character of our children can, therefore, be shaped in out schools.

Schools with both strong academic and character programs share certain similarities. They are places where children are both physically and psychologically safe and where care is taken to show respect for the building and its surroundings. They are places where teachers and staff are shown respect and, in turn, respect students. They are places that demonstrate an orientation to reach out to parents and community in a caring manner. And they are places where students are encouraged to behave in moral ways by offering direct services to their classmates and community.

Bibliography

Benninga, J. S., M. W. Berkowitz, P. Kuehn, and K. Smith. "The Relation of Character Education and Academic Achievement in California Elementary Schools." *Journal of Research in Character Education* 1.1 (2003): 17-30.

Damon, William. *Greater Expectations: Overcoming the Culture of Indulgence in America's Homes and Schools.* New York: Free Press, 1996.

Goleman, Daniel. *Emotional Intelligence: Why It Can Matter More Than IQ.* New York: Bantam, 1995.

Sherman, Nancy. "Educating the Stoic Warrior," in William Damon, ed., *Bringing in a New Era in Character Education.* Stanford, CA: Hoover Institution Press, 2002.

To the Teacher

Character education has been an aspect of American education since the early days of this country. Recently it has re-emerged as an important part of the goals of American education. Character education in social studies is a natural match. The content of social studies provides ample opportunity to examine character traits and the impact of character on people's lives.

In this booklet you will find emphasis on five character traits: citizenship, justice and fairness, respect, responsibility, and trustworthiness. Each of the five traits has an introductory lesson, which includes a lesson plan for the teacher and student handout sheets. These are followed by lists correlated to each of these books: *World History: Ancient Civilizations; World History: Medieval and Early Modern Times; Creating America: A History of the United States; Creating America: Beginnings through World War I; World History: Patterns of Interaction (survey); Modern World History; The Americans (survey);* and *The Americans: Reconstruction to the 21st Century.* Each list cites locations where examples of the trait are covered by the content. Each entry has an application activity. Other teacher materials include blackline masters listing all five traits and one linking the traits to each other, parent newsletters, student assessment forms, and a list of resources.

LESSON PLANS

The lesson plans for each trait can be used alone or as an introductory lesson to a unit. The lesson plan includes objectives, suggestions for focusing and motivating the study of a trait, a group activity, a writing assignment, and two blackline master handouts.

CORRELATED LISTS

To use these lists, select the trait you wish to emphasize and find the list for your textbook. The activities may be for individual students, small groups, or the entire class. In the lists, C stands for Chapter, L for lesson, and S for section.

BLACKLINE MASTERS

This booklet includes blackline masters showing the characteristics of each trait and the characteristics linked together. Each can be used to supplement instruction on the traits.

FAMILY LETTERS

Good instruction always includes links to the family. Each character trait lesson plan includes a letter to the family. The letter gives a definition of the character trait, suggested talking points, and a family activity to practice or explore the character trait.

STUDENT ASSESSMENT FORMS

Forms to help you evaluate student performance in cooperative activities as well as group discussions are included.

ADDITIONAL RESOURCES

A list of service and educational organizations is provided.

Linking The Traits

The five traits selected for study in this book can be linked together. The traits and their characteristics complement each other. You may want to devote some time to exploring the links suggested below.

Linking the Traits Lesson Plan

OBJECTIVES

1. Identify the connections between selected traits.
2. Identify common elements in all five traits.

SUGGESTED LINKAGES

Respect and Justice
Respect and Trustworthiness
Responsibility and Respect
Responsibility and Justice
Responsibility and Trustworthiness
Citizenship and Respect
Citizenship and Responsibility
Citizenship and Trustworthiness
Citizenship and Justice

FOCUS AND MOTIVATE

- Ask students if they think the character traits can be linked in a meaningful way. Discuss.
- Use the blackline master "Linking the Traits" to identify several traits you wish to link.

INSTRUCT

- Ask small groups of students to look at the elements of the traits selected on the blackline master "Five Character Traits" and identify any elements that are similar. Remind them that the words to not need to be identical but the ideas should be similar. For example, in Responsibility and Justice, obeying the law and playing by the rules are similar.
- Then have students look at other elements of the selected traits to see if they are complementary or contradictory. For example, in Citizenship and Responsibility, commitment to the community and obligations to the community are similar.
- Ask students to discuss ways in which the traits reinforce each other.
- Finally, have students illustrate their understanding of the linkages by creating one of the following: a poster or other art, a graphic organizer, a skit, or a plan for a multimedia production.

Five Character Traits

Citizenship

- Majority rule—minority rights
- Respect for authority
- Commitment to the community—family, city, state, nation
- Rights and responsibilities
- Patriotism

Justice/Fairness

- Equality for all
- Open-mindedness
- Playing by the rules

Respect

- Worth of self, family, friends, community, and environment
- Tolerance
- Peaceful conflict resolution

Responsibility

- Accountability
- Self-control
- Obligations to self, family, friends, community, and nations
- Obeying the law
- Citizen duties—voting, paying taxes, serving on a jury

Trustworthiness

- Honesty
- Dependability
- Loyalty
- Moral Convictions

Linking The Traits

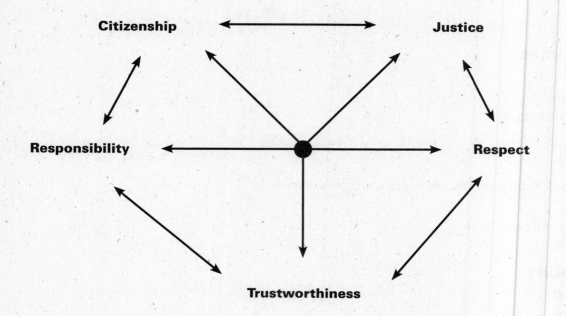

Citizenship

Justice

Responsibility

Respect

Trustworthiness

Citizenship

Citizenship is one of the basic components of good character. There are many elements to citizenship. In a society we agree to live by the rule of the majority, but the majority also agrees that the minority group has rights that cannot be taken away. A good citizen agrees to respect the authority of those who are in official positions. However, if those officials abuse their positions, the citizen has a right to object.

One of the most important elements of citizenship is commitment to the community. A community can be a family, a classroom, a city or town, a state, or a nation. Everyone lives with others. For a community to work well, all must cooperate and work to help one another. Sometimes this is called working for the common good, because everyone benefits from this cooperative effort.

All citizens have both rights and responsibilities. In the United States, the U.S. Constitution and the laws of the land guarantee our rights. Our responsibilities are also outlined there.

Finally, a good citizen loves his or her country and is willing to defend the land. This is called patriotism. Patriotism is more than waving a flag and singing the national anthem. It means being loyal to the country and working hard to make sure that all people in the land are treated well and fairly.

Citizenship Lesson Plan

OBJECTIVES	
	1. Define the concept of citizenship.
	2. Identify actions from daily life consistent with good citizenship.
	3. Study historical examples of individuals exhibiting good citizenship.

FOCUS AND MOTIVATE	
	• Have students complete the self-evaluation quiz on the handout sheet, page 9.
	• Review the questions and ask the students which three questions are about undesirable behaviors. *(6, 8, 9)* Discuss why they are undesirable. Discuss the idea of civil disobedience in relation to question 8.

INSTRUCT	**Part 1**
	• Tell students that you are investigating the character trait of citizenship. Ask them to come up with a definition.
	• Write the class definition on the board and compare it with the *American Heritage Student Dictionary* definition of **citizenship**: "The status of a citizen with its attendant duties, rights, and privileges."
	• Tell the class that being a responsible citizen requires you to understand that you are a part of a larger group, and because you are, you have certain rights and responsibilities.
	• Use the handout, page 10, to discuss these concepts.

Part 2

- Have the students silently read and react to the situation on the handout, page 10.
- Discuss the situation and ask students to share their responses.
- Ask which of the elements of citizenship this example deals with. *(commitment to community)*
- Ask students about their obligations—to self, family, friends, country.
- Discuss the consequences of failing to meet obligations to any of the above.
- Point out that a good citizen has a responsibility to help the community.
- Point out that in the course of studying history this year, they will encounter people whose lives showed what it means to be a good citizen.

Part 3

- Have the students silently read and react to the Thomas Jefferson statement found on the handout, page 9.
- Discuss and clarify if necessary the concept of commitment to community as seen in Jefferson's statement.
- Then ask why they think Jefferson would think being responsible for people in a society was important.
- Point out that not only elected leaders but also all citizens have a special obligation to their communities. Tell them that in studying history this year, they will encounter leaders and will study their behaviors to find examples of good citizenship.

GROUP ACTIVITY Divide the class into small groups. Have each group create a skit portraying both good and bad citizenship. The groups should perform their skits for the class.

WRITING ASSIGNMENT Write a composition describing what happens in a community when people don't practice the elements of good citizenship.

FAMILY NEWSLETTER Send out the family newsletter on the topic of citizenship. See page 52.

TEACHER NOTES
- Consult the tables on pages 11–15 to find examples of individuals exhibiting good citizenship in the following texts:
- *World History: Ancient Civilizations*
- *World History: Medieval and Early Modern Times*
- *Creating America: A History of the United States*
- *Creating America: Beginnings through World War I*
- *World History: Patterns of Interaction (survey)*
- *Modern World History*
- *The Americans (survey)*
- *The Americans: Reconstruction to the 21st Century*

Are You a Good Citizen?

PART 1

Try this quiz to see if you are a good citizen. Circle the number that best expresses
how you feel about the statement.

Agree	Sometimes Agree	Disagree	Don't Know
3	2	1	0

1. I obey the school and classroom rules. **3 2 1 0**

2. I work with the people in my community to make it a good place to live. **3 2 1 0**

3. I know the words to the pledge of allegiance. **3 2 1 0**

4. I help take care of the environment in my community. **3 2 1 0**

5. If I see someone in need I try to find someone to help him or her. **3 2 1 0**

6. I only look out for myself. Others can do the same. **3 2 1 0**

7. If I am on the winning side of a game or debate, I respect the losers. **3 2 1 0**

8. If a rule or law is unfair it is okay to break it. **3 2 1 0**

9. Since I am not an adult I do not need to worry about citizenship. **3 2 1 0**

10. I speak up if something is unfair. **3 2 1 0**

Study the statements. Which ones do you think illustrate good citizenship? Which
statements do you think concern questionable behavior? Consider how you scored
on these two sets of statements. Based on your scores, how well do you think you
understand what it means to be a good citizen?

PART 2

Read the paragraph below and write a sentence telling what you would do.

An empty lot near your home is filled with trash, cans and bottles, and
weeds. Rats and mice live and breed there. You think it would make a nice
tot lot if only somebody would clean it up. What, if anything, would you do
to reach your goal of getting a tot lot in your neighborhood?

_____

_____

PART 3

President Thomas Jefferson once wrote to a friend, "A nation as a society, forms a moral
person, and every member of it is personally responsible for his society." Tell what you
think Jefferson meant by this and why he thought it was important.

_____

_____

Citizenship

Citizenship is one of the basic components of good character. There are many elements to citizenship. In a society we agree to live by the rule of the majority, but the majority also agrees that the minority group has rights that cannot be taken away. A good citizen agrees to respect the authority of those who are in official positions. However, if those officials abuse their positions, the citizen has a right to object.

One of the most important elements of citizenship is commitment to the community. A community can be a family, a classroom, a city or town, a state, or a nation. Everyone lives with others. For a community to work well, all must cooperate and work to help one another. Sometimes this is called working for the common good, because everyone benefits from this cooperative effort.

All citizens have both rights and responsibilities. In the United States, the U.S. Constitution and the laws of the land guarantee our rights. Our responsibilities are also outlined there.

Finally, a good citizen loves his or her country and is willing to defend the land. This is called patriotism. Patriotism is more than waving a flag and singing the national anthem. It means being loyal to the country and working hard to make sure that all people in the land are treated well and fairly.

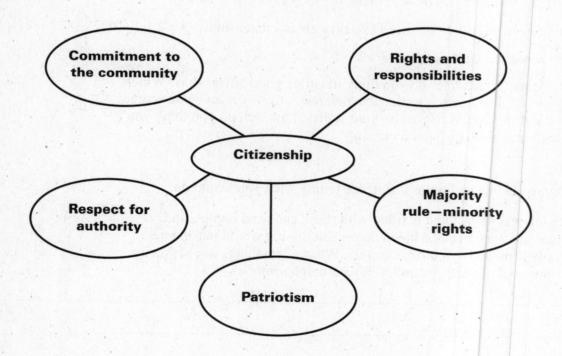

World History: Ancient Civilizations

Location	Topic/Person	Activity
C-2, L3	Need for law	Students discuss what would happen in a school if there were no rules. Then discuss why there is a need for government and for laws in a society.
C-4, L1	Rule of law	Students discuss what a code of laws has to do with rights and responsibilities of citizenship in a community.
C-4, L2	Type of government	Students create a Venn diagram showing the similarities and differences between living in a democracy and living in an empire.
C-6, L2 Primary Source	Goals of government	Students determine why King Ezana would choose these goals outlined in the Primary Source on p. 199. Ask what goals they would set if they were in a position of power in a community.
C-8, L2	Styles of government rule	Small groups of students create a poster showing how each Chinese philosophy would influence respect for authority and cooperation in a community.
C-10, L1 Primary Source	Ten Commandments	Students review the Ten Commandments and determine which commandments suggest a commitment to a community and explain in what way the commandment does so.
C-11, L4	Athenian democracy	Small groups create a poster showing the ways in which Athenian democracy was different from democracy as practiced in the United States.
C-12, L1	Citizenship	Students discuss the differences in the qualifications for citizenship as shown in the Venn diagram on p. 395. Then have them do research on how an individual can become a naturalized U.S. citizen.
C-13, L2	Civic duties	Students discuss how U.S. citizens show civic duty. Then ask whether there should be additional duties or if the three listed should be changed.
C-15, L1	Civic responsibility	Students identify failures in civic duty and the consequences of those failures as shown in the information under the heading "Political and Social Problems."

World History: Medieval and Early Modern Times

Location	Topic	Activity
C-2, L2	Civic responsibility	Students look at the chart on p. 56 and identify Romans' failure to fulfill civic duty. Ask students to look up the definition of *patriotism* and discuss what it means to them today.
C-2, L4	Laws	Students determine why the principles listed under the heading "Roman Law and Rights" are important to the ideas of rule of law and respect for authority.
C-3, L2	Five Pillars	Students look at the chart on p. 95 and determine which of the Five Pillars is related to sense of community. Discuss why compassion is a part of being in a community.
C-5, L3 Primary Source	Muslim rule	Students read the Primary Source on p. 167 and explain how the information reflects the impact of the rule of law and respect for authority in Mali.
C-7, L1	Confucianism	Small groups of students create a poster showing how following Confucianism would influence respect for authority and cooperation in a community.
C-8, L3	Military society	Students list advantages and disadvantages of living in a military society.
C-9, L1	Feudalism	Students write a paragraph agreeing or disagreeing with the idea that feudalism is an example of commitment to the community.
C-10, L4 Primary Source	Magna Carta	Students write a paragraph explaining why the Magna Carta is an example of the rule of law.
C-10, L4	Expansion of democracy	Small groups of students create a poster illustrating the changes in political ideas as shown in the section "Rise of Modern Democratic Thought."
C-14, L3	Protestantism and democracy	Students summarize the information that applies to the ideas of democracy and to citizenship in the material under the heading "Protestantism and Democracy." Ask how the Mayflower Compact reflects the elements of citizenship.
C-16, L1	Enlightenment ideas	Students create a chart listing Enlightenment philosophers, the philosophers' ideas, and how these ideas are reflected in American democratic practices.
C-16, L2	Expansion of democracy	Students create a chart or poster showing the expansion of democratic principles.

Creating America

A History of the United States	Beginnings through World War I	Topic	Activity
C-3, S3 Primary Source	C-3, S3 Primary Source	Mayflower Compact and Fundamental Orders of Connecticut	Students explain how the Mayflower Compact and the Fundamental Orders of Connecticut reflect the elements of citizenship.
C-5, S2 One American's Story	C-5, S2 One American's Story	Rights of Englishmen	Students explain how Increase Mather's actions show a commitment to the community. Then have students make a list of ways they could show their commitment to their community.
C-6, S4 Primary Source	C-6, S4 Primary Source	Declaration of Independence	Write the following phrases on the board: Rule of the Majority, Respect for Authority, Cooperation, Commitment to the Community. Use the A Closer Look boxes to help students find examples of these ideas in the Declaration of Independence.
C-8	C-8	The Constitution	Small groups of students find examples of how the Constitution incorporated these ideas: Rule of the Majority, Respect for Authority, Cooperation, Commitment to the Community. Each group should be prepared to report on its findings.
C-12, S1	C-12, S1	Jacksonian democracy	Students list ways that Jacksonian democracy expanded democratic rights in the United States. Then ask which groups at this time still do not have all their rights.
C-14, S3, 4	C-14, S3, 4	Reforming American society	Hold a class discussion on the idea of building a community by showing compassion. Have small groups make a chart listing the reformers in Sections 3 and 4 and identifying their activities.
C-18, S2	C-18, S2	KKK	Students identify reasons why the KKK is clearly not an example of good citizenship.
C-24, S3	C-24, S3	Patriotism	Students list patriotic actions shown in the material under the heading "Mobilizing for War." Then discuss how citizens show patriotism today.
C-29		Civil rights reforms	Small groups make a chart listing the reformers in the chapter and identifying their activities.

Note: the Citizenship Handbook and the Citizenship Today features will also provide material for studying citizenship.

World History: Patterns of Interaction

Survey	Modern World History	Topic	Activity
C-2, S1		Rule of law	Students discuss what they think will happen in a community with a code of laws. Ask students what a code of laws has to do with rights and responsibilities of citizenship in a community.
C-4, S4		Styles of government rule	Small groups of students create a poster showing how each Chinese philosophy would influence respect for authority and cooperation in a community.
C-5, S3	Prologue, S1	Citizenship	Students discuss the differences in the qualifications for citizenship as shown in the Venn diagram on p. 134. Then have them do research on how an individual can become a naturalized U.S. citizen.
C-6, S4		Civic duty	Students look at the chart on p. 174 and identify Romans' failure to fulfill civic duty in political, social, and military affairs. Ask students to look up the definition of *patriotism* and discuss what it means to them today.
C-14, S3	Prologue S3	Magna Carta	Students determine which of the following elements of citizenship are addressed in the Magna Carta: Rule of the Majority, Respect for Authority, Cooperation, Commitment to the Community. Have students explain their answers.
C-18, S1 History Maker	C-2, S1	Suleyman's law code	Students explain how Suleyman's law code addresses Respect for Authority, Cooperation, Commitment to the Community.
C-22, S2	C-6, S2	Enlightenment ideas	Small groups of students create a poster illustrating Enlightenment ideas as shown in the chart on major ideas of the Enlightenment.
C-23, S2	C-7, S2	Declaration of the Rights of Man	Provide students with a copy of the Rights of Man. Review the principles of the document and how it reflects the elements of citizenship.
C-26, S1	C-10, S1	Expansion of suffrage	Students study the graphs on suffrage in Britain and draw comparisons with U.S. suffrage.
C-34	C-18	Expansion of democracy	Small groups study each of the nations shown on the visual summary on p. 1028 and identify the challenges to building that nation.
C-35, S1	C-19, S1	Democratic practices	Small groups devise a way to show the information on the chart on p. 1033 in a different manner.

The Americans

Survey	Reconstruction to the 21st Century	Topic	Activity
C-2	G-1, S2, S3	Establishing community and citizenship goals	Students identify events that exemplify each of the following traits of citizenship: Rule of the Majority, Respect for Authority, Cooperation, Commitment to the Community.
C-4, S2	C-2, S1	Declaration of Independence	Write the following phrases on the board: Rule of the Majority, Respect for Authority, Cooperation, Commitment to the Community. Ask students to find examples of these ideas in the Declaration of Independence.
The Constitution	The Constitution	Bill of Rights and the amendments	Students make a list of the rights guaranteed in the Bill of Rights and the amendments. Discuss how the nature of citizenship expanded.
C-8, S3	C-3, S5	Women reformers	Students examine the role of women in 19th-century reform movements. Ask how these movements fit into the element of commitment to community.
C-10, S4	C-4, S1	Secession of the Southern states	Students discuss the following statement: "Thinking about the rule of majority, respect for the minority, commitment to community, and cooperation, I believe that the secession of the South was justified."
C-12, S1	C-4, S4	Reconstruction legislation	Students create a poster illustrating how Reconstruction legislation expanded the rights of citizenship.
C-15, S1	C-7, S1	Immigration	Students determine if American schools became a vehicle for patriotism during this era. Ask if they think this was appropriate. Next ask how patriotism can be instilled in the 21st century.
C-17, S1	C-9, S1	Political corruption	Students engage in a discussion about why it is important to clean up political corruption. Ask students to find examples of modern-day corruption.
C-23, S2	C-14, S2	Depression era legislation	Students determine which of the New Deal agencies fit into theses elements of citizenship: Commitment to the Community or Compassion
C-29	C-21	Civil rights	Students construct a chart listing leaders in the civil rights movements and their accomplishments.
C-33, S3	C-25, S3	1980s social concerns	Students discuss how action on social concerns issues reflects the Commitment to Community element of citizenship.

Justice

Justice is one basic component of good character. Justice and fairness are two sides of the same coin. When a person acts in a fair manner toward others, he or she is showing justice. When a country or a leader acts in a fair manner, we call it justice. A fair, or just, person is open-minded. Such a person listens to others and studies all sides of an issue before making a judgment about it.

Practicing fairness and justice means that everyone is considered equal. In daily life this means you play by the rules, take turns, and share. In a just society, no one has an advantage over another person.

Supporting fairness and justice also means taking action to support those ideas in your community. Fair and just leaders and countries work to make life good for everyone.

Justice Lesson Plan

OBJECTIVES	**1.** Define the concept of justice.
	2. Identify actions consistent with the definition of justice.
	3. Study historical examples of individuals acting in a just or fair way.
FOCUS AND MOTIVATE	• Have students complete the self-evaluation quiz on the handout sheet, page 18.
	• Review the questions and ask students which two questions are about undesirable behaviors *(2,8)*. Discuss why they are undesirable. Also, ask students to discuss if questions 4 and 9 represent just or fair attitudes. Have them explain their responses.
INSTRUCT	**Part 1**
	• Tell students that you are investigating the character trait of justice, or fairness. Ask them to come up with a definition.
	• Write the class definition on the board and compare it with the *American Heritage Student Dictionary* definition of **justice:** "The quality of being fair."
	• Tell the class that being a fair, or just, person requires you to play by the rules, treat all people equally, and listen to the point of view of others. Discuss these concepts. Have students consider situations in which it might be acceptable to actually give someone an advantage and not treat them equally. (i.e. people with physical or mental challenges, those who do not understand the language, etc.)
	Part 2
	• Have the students silently read and react to the situation on the handout, page 18.
	• Discuss the situation and ask students to share their responses.
	• Ask which aspect of justice this example deals with. *(fairness to other students in the line)*
	• Ask students with whom they should be fair, or just—self, family, friends, country.
	• Discuss the consequences of failing to be fair, or just, to any one of the above.

Part 2 *(continued)*

- Ask students why a leader or country should be just.
- Point out that in the course of studying history this year, they will encounter some leaders and countries who were fair and just and others who were not.

Part 3

- Have the students silently read and react to the Theodore Roosevelt statement found on the handout, page 18.
- Discuss and clarify if necessary the concept of fairness and justice as seen in Roosevelt's statement.
- Ask what conditions in a country would influence Roosevelt to make this statement.
- Finally ask if the ideas of justice and fairness can be applied to relationships between countries. Discuss the concept of just and fair treatment between nations.
- Point out that elected leaders have a special obligation to be accountable for their behavior. Tell them that in studying history this year, they will encounter leaders and will study their behaviors to see if they were just leaders.

GROUP ACTIVITY	Divide the class into small groups. Each group should create lists of things they think are unfair at school and in the community or the nation. Next they should compare their lists with those of other groups in the class. Finally, come up with a list in each category that fits all groups. Have the small groups brainstorm ways to solve the unfair issues raised.
WRITING ASSIGNMENT	Write a short story using the theme of justice or fairness.
FAMILY NEWSLETTER	Send out the family newsletter on the topic of justice. See page 53.
TEACHER NOTES	Consult the tables on pages 20–24 to find examples of individuals exhibiting good citizenship in the following texts:

- Consult the tables on pages 11–15 to find examples of individuals exhibiting good citizenship in the following texts:
- *World History: Ancient Civilizations*
- *World History: Medieval and Early Modern Times*
- *Creating America: A History of the United States*
- *Creating America: Beginnings through World War I*
- *World History: Patterns of Interaction (survey)*
- *Modern World History*
- *The Americans (survey)*
- *The Americans: Reconstruction to the 21st Century*

How Fair are You?

PART 1

Try this quiz to see if you are a fair person. Circle the number that best expresses how you feel about the statement.

Agree	Sometimes Agree	Disagree	Don't Know
3	2	1	0

1. I listen to what others say before judging them.   **3   2   1   0**

2. When I want to win, I ignore the game's rules.   **3   2   1   0**

3. I try to think of the feelings of others when I act.   **3   2   1   0**

4. The strongest people should always win.   **3   2   1   0**

5. What my friends say about someone else is important to me.   **3   2   1   0**

6. To be treated fairly you should treat others fairly.   **3   2   1   0**

7. There is never a time in which someone should get an extra advantage.   **3   2   1   0**

8. Some people deserve to be taken advantage of.   **3   2   1   0**

9. The smartest people should always win.   **3   2   1   0**

10. I am good at following rules.   **3   2   1   0**

Study the statements. Which ones do you think illustrate fairness? Which statements do you think concern questionable behavior? Consider how you scored on these two sets of statements. Based on your scores, do you think you qualify as a fair person?

PART 2

Read the paragraph below and write a sentence telling what you would do.

> Just before lunch, your teacher asked you to stay after class to talk about an assignment. Your friends went to the lunchroom without you. When you get there, you see the lunch line is very long because everyone's favorite meal is being served. You see that your friends are still in line. Will you try to cut into the line with your friends or wait your turn?

_____

_____

PART 3

President Theodore Roosevelt said, "This country will not be a good place for any of us to live in unless we make it a good place for all of us to live in." Tell what you think this statement has to do with being fair and just.

_____

_____

Justice

Justice is one basic aspect of good character. Justice and fairness are two sides of the same coin. When a person acts in a fair manner toward others, he or she is showing justice. When a country or a leader acts in a fair manner, we call it justice. A fair, or just, person is open-minded. Such a person listens to others and studies all sides of an issue before making a judgment about it.

Practicing fairness and justice means that everyone is considered equal. In daily life this means you play by the rules, take turns, and share. In a just society, no one has an advantage over another person.

Supporting fairness and justice also means taking action to support those ideas in your community. Fair and just leaders and countries work to make life good for everyone.

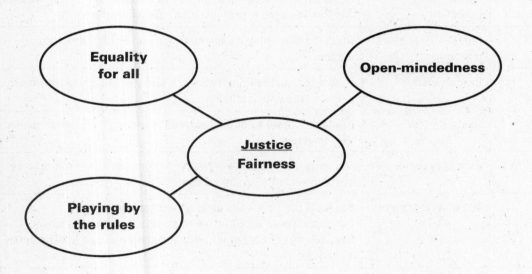

World History: Ancient Civilizations

Location	Topic	Activity
C-3, L2	Living in cities	Students discuss how living in a city calls for using some of the traits of fairness.
C-4, Starting with a Story	Need for laws	Students create a list of the kinds of behaviors in school that make laws (rules) necessary.
C-4, L1	Hammurabi	Students research the Code of Hammurabi to determine what types of behaviors were regulated by the code and create a poster illustrating some of the regulated acts.
C-4, L2	Assyrian control	Students discuss the Assyrian treatment of captured people. Ask how the harsh treatment would make people feel and respond.
C-4, L3	Cyrus' policy of toleration	Students write a comparison-and-contrast essay on the Assyrian and Persian concepts of justice as shown by the chart.
C-5, L4	Ramses' peace treaty	Students determine if a peace treaty can insure fairness or justice.
C-6, L2 Primary Source	Ezana's pledge	Students read the Primary Source and discuss Ezana's desire to live in peace with justice.
C-7, L2	Caste system	Students create a political cartoon reflecting their views on the caste system.
C-8, S2	Ethical systems	Students use a graphic organizer to compare views of the three systems on fairness and justice.
C-10, S1 Primary Source	Ten Commandments	Students create a Venn diagram comparing the Ten Commandments with the five relationships in Confucianism. Discuss the concept of fairness and justice shown in each set of directives.
C-11, L3	Forms of government	Students study the forms of government chart and determine in which form an individual would most likely be treated more fairly, or justly.
C-12, L2	Pericles and Delian League	Students write a letter to Pericles protesting his unfair treatment of the other city-states.
C-13, L1	Roman Tribal Assembly	Students discuss the tribal assembly and determine if it could help bring fairness to Roman life.
C-13, L2	Caesar's reforms	Students role-play a situation in which Caesar argues for his reforms with members of the Roman Senate.
C-15, L3	Justinian's Code	Students research Justinian's Code and prepare a brief oral report about it.

World History: Medieval and Early Modern Times

Location	Topic	Activity
C-2, L4	Roman law	Students look at the U.S. Constitution, Amendments, 4-6 and determine which two principles of Roman law are found there.
C-2, L3	Justinian's Code	Students research Justinian's Code and prepare a brief oral report about it.
C-3, L2	People of the Book	Students discuss why the policy of toleration is just. Remind them of the policies of Cyrus studied in the previous year.
C-4, L2	Abbasid's policy of inclusion	Students discuss the advantages of a policy of inclusion. Then have small groups of students role-play a situation in which inclusion is called into question.
C-5, L2 Primary Source	Justice in Mali	Students identify the results of justice within a country after reading the Primary Source.
C-7, L1	Taizong's rule	Students discuss why Taizong's rule was considered fair and just by the peasants. Why might the nobles have felt differently?
C-9, L2	Guilds	Students identify how a guild could promote fairness both for its members and for buyers of its products. Students research a labor union to see how the organization helps promote fairness for its members and for consumers.
C-10, L2	Inquisition	Students list ways the Inquisition of Ferdinand and Isabella is an example of injustice. Then students research the Inquisition and list reasons why the Inquisition was unfair and unjust.
C-10, L4 Primary Source	Magna Carta	Students study the U.S. Constitution to find examples of the protected rights *(Art 1, Section 8.1, Amendments 5, 6, 7, 14)* and compare them with information about the Magna Carta.
C-12, L1, 2	Strict societies	Students decide if the societies in Lessons 1 and 2 described as strict seem to be just, or fair. Students should give reasons for their answers.
C-13, L3	Printing press	Small groups of students create a poster or collage identifying ways in which the printed word enhances fairness and justice.
C-16, L1	Enlightenment thinkers	Small groups of students create a chart to show Enlightenment thinkers and their ideas. Discuss how these ideas influence ideas about justice and fairness.
C-17, L12	Rights of Man, Rights of Woman	Divide the class in half. Pair students in each half. Pairs of students in one half research the *Declaration of the Rights of Man*; the other half researches *A Vindication of the Rights of Woman*. Research should focus on the concept of justice. Pairs from each half share their findings with pairs from the other half.

Creating America

A History of the United States	Beginnings through World War I	Topic	Activity
C-2, S3	C-2, S3	The New Laws 1542	Students role-play a discussion between the Spanish king and Spanish colonists about the New Laws.
C-6 Primary Source	C-6 Primary Source	Declaration of Independence	Remind students that the Declaration was a statement of concern over injustice. Have students use the Declaration to identify some of the reasons the colonists were angry.
Constitution	Constitution	Bill of Rights and Amendments	Assign pairs of students one of the following amendments: 1-6, 13, 14, 15, 19, 23, 24, 26. Each pair should identify why their assigned amendment ensures justice.
C-12, S1	C-12, S1	Jacksonian democracy	Students study the chart on changes in ideas about democracy. Students take the information on the chart and put it into a different graphic form.
C-12, S2	C-12, S2	Indian Removal policy	Students debate the justice of Jackson's Removal policy.
C-14, S4	C-14, S4	Abolitionists and women's rights	Small groups of students create a mural showing the main abolitionists and women's rights reformers.
C-17, S1	C-17, S1	Emancipation Proclamation	Students create a newscast featuring President Lincoln's emancipation order and responses by supporters, opponents, and African-American slaves.
C-17, S4 PS	C-17, S4 PS	Lincoln's 2nd Inaugural Address	Students discuss how the thoughts expressed in the final paragraph of Lincoln's 2nd Inaugural Address reflect Lincoln's idea of justice.
C-18, S3	C-18, S3	Civil rights	Small groups of students study the chart on Reconstruction Civil Rights Amendments and Laws. Then they convert the basic information into a visual presentation.
C-21, S2	C-21, S2	Immigration restrictions	Students conduct a debate on the topic "It is fair to restrict immigration to save real Americans' jobs."
C-24, S3 One American's Story	C-24, S3 One American's Story	Women in the work force	Students discuss how wartime conditions can increase or decrease toleration and open-mindedness.
C-27, S4		Japanese-American internment	Students write a letter to the editor protesting the treatment of Japanese Americans.
C-28, S1		Truman's Fair Deal	Students use the Internet to research the proposed reforms in Truman's Fair Deal. Then they illustrate their findings in a collage or poster.
C-29		Civil rights	Students create a multimedia presentation, tracing the attempts to increase fairness and justice in American society.

World History: Patterns of Interaction

Survey	Modern World History	Topic	Activity
C-2, S1		Hammurabi	Students research the Code of Hammurabi to determine what types of behaviors were regulated by the code and create a poster illustrating some of the regulated acts.
C-3 Primary Source	Prologue S2	Ten Commandments	Students create a Venn diagram comparing the Ten Commandments with Hammurabi's Code. Discuss the concept of justice shown in each set of directives.
C-4, S4		Chinese ethical systems	Students study the chart on Chinese ethical systems and determine which system they think will provide the greatest justice for the land.
C-5, S3	Prologue S1	Athenian democracy	Students discuss the ways in which Athenian democracy extended the concept of justice.
C-6, S5	Prologue S1	Roman law	Students study the list of Roman law principles on page 183 and look for those principles in the United States Constitution.
C-14, S2		Guilds	Students identify how a guild could promote fairness both for its members and for buyers of its products. Students research a labor union to see how the organization helps promote fairness for its members and for consumers.
C-15, S1		Justice in stateless societies	Students role-play a situation in which justice is meted out using the traditional methods of stateless societies.
C-20, S2	C-4, S2	Bartolomé de Las Casas	Students write a letter to Las Casas either supporting or rejecting his stand on both the Indians and Africans.
C-23, S1	C-7, S1	French Revolution	Students study the information on the Three Estates chart and write a paragraph discussing the injustice of French society at the time of the French Revolution.
C-11, S2 Analyzing Key Concepts	C-11, S2	Imperialism	Students study the chart on Imperial management methods. Then discuss the impact each method might have on the justice that inhabitants of colonies using that method might receive.
C-30, S2	C-14, S2	Totalitarianism and justice	Students write a paragraph identifying the ways that totalitarianism prevents justice from occurring.
C-34, S5	C-18, S5	Afghanistan	Students list obstacles to justice that have existed or currently exist in Afghanistan.

The Americans

Survey	Reconstruction to the 21st Century	Topic	Activity
C-4, S1	C-2, S1	Colonial reactions to the British	Students use the action-reaction time line on pages 100-101 to identify the British acts that the colonists viewed as injustices and explain why they were viewed as injustices.
Constitution	Constitution	Amendments to increase justice	Students review the amendments to the Constitution and make a list of those amendments that increase the scope of justice in the United States. Discuss the students' selections.
C-7, S3		Indian Removal Act	Students read the Primary Source " The Cherokee Nation's Appeal to the American People" and write a one-paragraph response.
C-8, S2		Dorothea Dix	Students read the Primary Source on Dorothea Dix, "Report to the Massachusetts Legislature," and write a one-paragraph response.
C-10, S2	C-4, S2	Underground Railroad	Students discuss how the actions of individuals supporting the Underground Railroad represent a commitment to fairness and justice.
C-12, S1	C-4, S4	Reconstruction legislation	Students review the information shown in the chart on Major Reconstruction Legislation. Then they should identify and list ways in which the legislation brought fairness and justice to African-Americans.
C-14, S3	C-6, S3	Labor unions	Small groups of students create a poster showing how labor unions helped to bring fairness and justice to workers in the late 19th century.
C-17, S1	C-9, S1	Progressive movement	Students identify the ways in which the Progressive movement fought for fairness and justice.
C-22, S3	C-14, S3	Hoover and the Bonus Army	Divide the class in half. Assign one half the point of view of Hoover and the other the members of the Bonus Army. Debate the actions Hoover took in disbanding the Bonus Army.
C-25, S4	C-17, S4	Japanese-American internment	Students discuss the justice of the settlement actions taken to resolve claims made by Japanese Americans.
C-29	C-21	Civil Rights	Small groups of students keep a list of examples of respect or lack of it in this chapter. When the chapter is finished list all examples on the board and discuss.
C-31, S2	C-23, S2	Women's rights	Small groups create a poster illustrating examples of injustice women experienced.
C-32, S3	C-24, S3	Equal rights	Students study the chart showing the differences in wages between men and women to determine if the differences reflect an aspect of respect. Then have them check the current figures to determine if changes have occurred since the chart was created. Ask if they expect future changes.

Respect

Respect is one basic component of good character. Respect includes recognizing the worth and dignity of all people. It also involves self-respect, respect for the community, tolerance, and peaceful resolution of conflicts. Acting with respect allows us to live in peace and harmony in a society. A respectful person is considerate of others and makes every effort to regard each person as a valuable human being.

A respectful person understands that in every society people have disagreements. But she or he believes that those disagreements should be settled in a nonviolent manner. A respectful person does not belittle others. A respectful person does not bully others.

Respect Lesson Plan

OBJECTIVES
1. Define the concept of respect.
2. Identify actions consistent with the definition of respect.
3. Study historical examples of individuals exhibiting respectful behavior.

FOCUS AND MOTIVATE
- Have students complete the self-evaluation quiz on the handout sheet, page 27.
- Review the questions and ask the students which four questions are about undesirable behaviors. *(2,6,7,9)* Discuss why they are undesirable.

INSTRUCT

Part 1
- Tell students that you are investigating the character trait of respect. Ask them to come up with a definition.
- Write the class definition on the board and compare it with a dictionary definition. *The American Heritage Student Dictionary* defines **respect** as "to feel or show high regard for." Tell the class that being a respectful person requires you to be considerate, tolerant, and willing to resolve conflicts peaceably. Use the handout, page 28, to help in the discussion of these concepts.
- Remind students that respect encompasses self, family, friends, community, and the environment.

Part 2
- Have the students silently read and react to the situation on the handout sheet, page 27.
- Discuss the situation and ask students to share their responses.
- Ask which aspect of respect this example deals with. *(human worth and dignity)*
- Ask students to whom or what they should be respectful—self, family, friends, country.
- Discuss the consequences of failing to be respectful to any one of the above.
- Point out that in the course of studying history this year, they will encounter some people who were respectful and others who were not.

RESPECT LESSON PLAN CONTINUED

Part 3

- Have the students silently read and react to the John F. Kennedy statement found on the handout on page 27.
- Discuss and clarify if necessary the concept of respect as seen in Kennedy's statement.
- Then ask students why they think things either have improved since Kennedy's time, have stayed the same, or have gotten worse.
- Point out that elected leaders have a special obligation to be accountable for their behavior. Tell them that in studying history this year, they will encounter leaders and will study their behaviors to see if they were respectful leaders.

GROUP ACTIVITY   Divide the class into small groups. Have each group create a skit showing a way to resolve a conflict between two students who accidentally bumped into each other in the hallway. After they view the skits, have students discuss ways to solve problems peacefully.

WRITING ASSIGNMENT   Write a composition agreeing or disagreeing with the following statement: "I don't have to like you, but I can treat you with respect."

FAMILY NEWSLETTER   Send out the family newsletter on the topic of respect. See page 54.

TEACHER NOTES   Consult the tables on pages 29–33 to find examples of individuals exhibiting either respectful or disrespectful behavior in the following texts:

- *World History: Ancient Civilizations*
- *World History: Medieval and Early Modern Times*
- *Creating America: A History of the United States*
- *Creating America: Beginnings through World War I*
- *World History: Patterns of Interaction (survey)*
- *Modern World History*
- *The Americans (survey)*
- *The Americans: Reconstruction to the 21st Century*

Do You Act with Respect?

PART 1

Try this quiz to see how respectful you are. Circle the number that best expresses how you feel about the statement.

Agree	Sometimes Agree	Disagree	Don't Know
3	2	1	0

1. I respect myself.   **3   2   1   0**

2. If I disagree with someone, I will tell him or her in no uncertain terms.   **3   2   1   0**

3. If someone is bullying another person, I will tell him or her to stop.   **3   2   1   0**

4. I am considered a polite person with good manners.   **3   2   1   0**

5. Every person has the right to be treated respectfully.   **3   2   1   0**

6. Respecting the environment is not very important.   **3   2   1   0**

7. Some people don't deserve to be respected.   **3   2   1   0**

8. People should work out conflicts in a nonviolent way.   **3   2   1   0**

9. Practicing tolerance is not necessary.   **3   2   1   0**

10. People in my community are generally respectful.   **3   2   1   0**

Study the statements. Which ones do you think illustrate respectful behavior? Which statements do you think concern questionable behavior? Consider how you scored on these two sets of statements. Based on your scores, do you think you qualify as a respectful person?

PART 2

Read the paragraph below and write a sentence telling what you would do.

> There is a new student at your school. You must admit he is a little funny looking. But you don't think he deserves to be teased and embarrassed by other students. You overheard a group of students planning to grab him and stuff him in a locker. What do you do?

_____

_____

PART 3

In 1963, President John F. Kennedy said, "Every American ought to have the right to be treated as he would wish to be treated, as one would wish his children to be treated. This is not the case." Do you think that things in the United States have changed since 1963?

_____

_____

Respect

Respect is one basic part of good character. Respect includes recognizing the worth and dignity of all people. It also involves self-respect, respect for the community, tolerance, and peaceful resolution of conflicts. Acting with respect allows us to live in peace and harmony in a society. A respectful person is considerate of others and makes every effort to regard each person as a valuable human being.

A respectful person understands that in every society people have disagreements. But she or he believes that those disagreements should be settled in a nonviolent manner. A respectful person does not belittle others. A respectful person does not bully others.

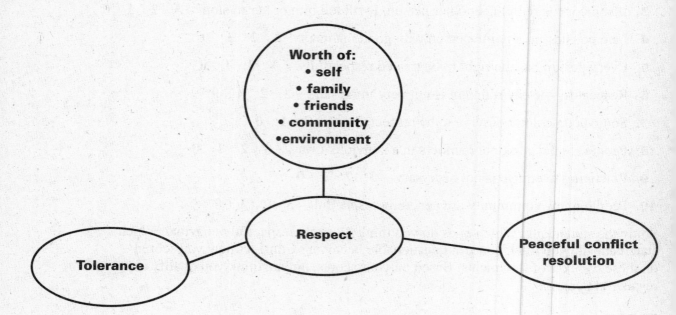

World History: Ancient Civilizations

Location	Topic	Activity
C-2, L1	Human communities	Students read the material under the heading "Early Human Culture." Then students decide how each of the aspects of culture listed there helped build community respect.
C-4, L1	Law codes	Students explain how law codes can create an atmosphere of respect in a community.
C-4, L3	Persian tolerance	Pairs of students devise a set of questions to ask Cyrus or Darius about their policies of toleration. Have pairs exchange the questions and try to answer them.
C-5, L4	Hittite treaty	Students identify ways the signing of a treaty between the Egyptians and the Hittites illustrates elements of respect.
C-7, L3	Rule of Asoka	Students read the material under the heading "Asoka, the Buddhist King" and identify policies that showed elements of respect.
C-8, L2	Legalism	Small groups of students discuss the level of respect shown by practicing legalism.
C-8, L2	Confucianism	Small groups of students create a poster showing the five relationships and the respect the teaching demands.
C-10 Primary Source	Ten Commandments	Students review the Ten Commandments to determine how the commandments create an atmosphere of respect in a community. Next, students compare the Ten Commandments with Hammurabi's Code studied in Chapter 4.
C-12, L1	Athenian democracy	Students write a paragraph about Athenian democracy showing how this form of government encourages both individual and community respect.
C-14, L2	Early Christian Church	Small groups of students create a collage or poster showing the groups of people who wanted to be a part of the Christian Church because of its tolerance.
C-15 Starting with a Story and L2	Germanic tribes	Students read the "Starting with a Story" and the material in Lesson 2 on the Germanic tribes. Students discuss why it was unfair of the Romans to judge the culture of the Germanic tribes. Ask what might have happened if the Romans had been more tolerant.

World History: Medieval and Early Modern Times

Location	Topic	Activity
C-2, L4	Roman law	Students write a paragraph about how Roman law and rights fostered respect.
C-3, L1	Arabic clans	Students discuss how the Arabic clans helped to establish self-worth and community respect.
C-3, L2	Muslim tolerance	Students discuss why Islamic teachings promote respect by Muslims for Christianity and Judaism.
C-4, L2	Abbasid power	Read the material under the heading "Abbasid Power." Then ask students if they think the Abbasid policy of tolerance was successful and why.
C-5, L1	African families	Students write a paragraph about how African village life fostered respect of self and of community after reading the material under the heading "Village in West Africa."
C-7, L1	Confucianism	Small groups of students create a poster showing Confucian principles and identifying the elements of respect in the principles.
C-9, L2	Guilds	Students do some research to find out how guilds helped to improve communities.
C-10, L5	Ottoman tolerance	Pairs of students list the ways that the Ottoman government was tolerant of people living in conquered communities.
C-13, L1	Humanist thought	Students discuss how the humanist thinkers encouraged the elements of respect.
C-13, L3	Impact of printing	Students create a poster showing how the printing press changed society's ideas about other people.
C-16, L4	Enlightenment ideas	Divide the class into four groups. Assign each group one of the following Enlightenment thinkers: Locke, Voltaire, Rousseau, Wollstonecraft. Have each group determine what ideas the thinker had about respect of self or of community. Then have each group share their findings with the other groups.

Creating America

A History of the United States	Beginnings through World War I	Topic	Activity
C-2, S3	C-2, S3	Native American resistance to Spanish	Small groups of students create a list of ways that the encounters between Native Americans and Spanish could have been handled to reduce bloodshed. Class may discuss the lists and decide if any of the suggestions would have worked.
C-6, S4	C-6, S4	Declaration of Independence	Tell students that the bulk of the Declaration contains colonial grievances against the king. Have them find the paragraph in the Declaration that shows the colonists attempt to address the grievances. Ask how the king showed his disrespect.
C-10, S3	C-10, S3	Tecumseh	Students read the information in the More About Tecumseh and read the material about Tecumseh under the heading "Tecumseh and Native American Unity." Then students identify elements of respect represented by Tecumseh.
C-14, S4	C-14, S4	Abolition and women's rights	Students write a paragraph on how the actions of abolitionists and women reformers were aimed at increasing respect for African Americans and women.
C-21, S3	C-21, S3	Washington and Du Bois	Small groups of students create a Venn diagram showing the similarities and differences in the ideas of Washington and Du Bois. Then they discuss the ways in which the ideas of these men helped to increase respect for self and community.
C-22, S1	C-22, S1	Roosevelt and conservation	Students write a paragraph on why Roosevelt's conservation measures were an example of respect for the environment.
C-25, S3		Harlem Renaissance	Small groups of students create a poster or collage showing how the Harlem Renaissance increased self-respect among African-Americans.
C-26, S2		New Deal	Small groups of students review the chart on major programs of the New Deal, then create a list categorizing programs that improve respect for self, community, and environment.
C-29		Civil rights movement	Small groups of students keep a list of examples of respect or lack of it in this chapter. When the chapter is finished, list all examples on the board and discuss.
C-31, S3		Environmental movement	Students discuss why the environmental movement is a reflection of respect. Continue the discussion with the Interdisciplinary Challenge activities.

World History: Patterns of Interaction

Survey	Modern World History	Topic	Activity
C-4, S3		Persian tolerance	Pairs of students devise a set of questions to ask Cyrus or Darius about their policies of tolerance. Have pairs exchange the questions and try to answer them.
C-7, S1		Asoka	Students identify policies that showed elements of respect after reading the material under the heading "Asoka Promotes Buddhism."
C-10, S2 Primary Source		Muslim tolerance of conquered people	Students read the Primary Source and discuss the elements of respect illustrated in it.
C-15, S1 Social History		African conflict resolution	Students read the information in the Social History sidebar. Use the information to set up a role-playing situation featuring a conflict resolution over a land.
C-20, S1	C-4, S1	Resistance to Spanish rule	Small groups of students create a list of ways that the encounters between Native Americans and the Spanish could have been handled to reduce bloodshed. Class may discuss the lists and decide if any of the suggestions would have worked.
C-22, S2	C-6, S2	Enlightenment ideas	Divide the class into four groups. Assign each group one of the following Enlightenment thinkers: Locke, Voltaire, Rousseau, and Wollstonecraft. Have each group determine what ideas the thinker had about respect of self or of community. Then have each group share their findings with the other groups.
C-23, S2	C-7, S2	Declaration of the Rights of Man and of the Citizen	Small groups of students do additional research on the Declaration of the Rights of Man and of the Citizen and create a poster illustrating the elements of respect found in the document.
C-28, S4	C-12, S4	Benito Juárez	Students write a paragraph summarizing the actions of Benito Juárez and link them to elements of respect.
C-29, S4	C-13, S4	Treaty of Versailles	Have students list the ways that the Treaty of Versailles disrespected nations or people.
C-34, S4	C-18, S4	Arab-Israeli conflict	Small groups of students discuss how the lack of respect on both sides of the Arab-Israeli conflict undermines efforts to bring peace to the region.

The Americans

Survey	Reconstruction to the 21st Century	Topic	Activity
C-2, S3	C-1, S3	Native American resistance to colonists	Small groups of students create a list of ways that the encounters between Native Americans and colonists could have been handled to reduce bloodshed. Class may discuss the lists and decide if any of the suggestions would have worked.
C-4, S2	C-2, S1	Declaration of Independence	Tell students that the bulk of the Declaration contains colonial grievances against the king. Have them find the paragraph in the Declaration that shows the colonists' attempt to address the grievances. Ask how the king showed his disrespect of English tradition.
C-7, S1		Sectionalism	Students discuss the policy of sectionalism and determine if it created a climate of respect between the parties.
C-12, S2	C-4, S4	Reconstruction	Students identify which programs of Reconstruction were designed to increase self-respect and which were oriented toward respecting the community.
C-15, S1	C-7, S1	"Melting pot"	Students debate the question of whether a melting pot respects or disrespects self and ethnic identities. If time, move on to discuss the "salad theory" and its impact on respect.
C-17, S3	C-9, S3	Roosevelt and conservation	Students write a paragraph on why Roosevelt's conservation measures were an example of respect for the environment.
C-19, S4	C-11, S4	Treaty of Versailles	Students list the ways the Treaty of Versailles disrespected nations or people.
C-21, S4	C-13, S4	Harlem Renaissance	Small groups of students create a poster or collage showing how the Harlem Renaissance increased self-respect among African-Americans.
C-26, S2	C-18, S2	MacArthur vs. Truman	Students identify how MacArthur's behavior was an example of both personal disrespect and disrespect of the office of the president.
C-28, S2	C-20, S3	Great Society programs	Small groups of students review the Great Society programs on p. 896. Each group should create a list categorizing programs that improve respect for self, community, and environment.
C-32, S3	C-25, S3	Equal rights	Students study the chart showing the differences in wages between men and women to determine if the differences reflect an aspect of respect. Then have them check the current figures to determine if changes have occurred since the chart was created. Ask if they expect future changes.

Responsibility

Responsibility is one basic component of good character. Responsibility includes both accountability and obligation. A responsible person is accountable for his or her actions. This means taking the credit when it is deserved and the blame when it is deserved. A responsible person does not pass the blame to someone else when things go wrong. He or she recognizes that an action has caused problems or inconvenience to someone else.

A responsible person also recognizes obligations to self, family, community, state, and nation. Personal responsibility includes exercising self-control and taking care of one's self and family. Civic responsibilities involve obeying the law; respecting the rights of others; and participating in the life of the community by voting, paying taxes, and serving on juries.

Responsibility Lesson Plan

OBJECTIVES	**1.** Define the concept of responsibility.
	2. Identify actions from daily life consistent with the definition of responsibility.
	3. Study historical examples of individuals exhibiting responsibility..
FOCUS AND MOTIVATE	• Have students complete the self-evaluation quiz on the handout sheet, page 36.
	• Review the questions and ask the students which two questions are about undesirable behaviors. *(3,6)* Discuss why they are undesirable.
INSTRUCT	**Part 1**
	• Tell students that you are investigating the character trait of responsibility. Ask them to come up with a definition.
	• Write the class definition on the board and compare it with a dictionary definition. *The American Heritage Student Dictionary* defines **responsibility** as "the quality or state of being dependable or accountable."
	• Tell the class that being a responsible person requires you to be accountable and to recognize you have certain obligations.
	• Use the handout, page 37, to discuss these concepts.
	Part 2
	• Have the students silently read and react to the situation on the handout, page 36.
	• Discuss the situation and ask students to share their responses.
	• Ask which of the aspects of responsibility this example deals with. *(obligation)*
	• Ask students to whom or what they have obligations—self, family, friends, country.
	• Discuss the consequences of failing to meet obligations to any one of the above.
	• Point out that in the course of studying history this year, they will encounter people who fulfilled their obligations to others.

Part 3

- Have the students silently read and react to Harry Truman's statement found on the handout sheet, page 36.
- Discuss and clarify if necessary the concept of accountability as seen in Truman's statement.
- Then ask why they think Truman would have this statement on his desk.
- Point out that elected leaders have a special obligation to be accountable for their behavior. Tell them that in studying history this year, they will encounter leaders and will study their behaviors to see if they were responsible leaders.

GROUP ACTIVITY	Divide the class into small groups. Have each group put together a list of actions—both what to do and what not to do—for a responsible person. Then the group should illustrate their list on a large sheet of paper or poster board.
WRITING ASSIGNMENT	Write a composition describing what responsibilities you have toward yourself, your family, your community, and the world.
FAMILY NEWSLETTER	Send out the family newsletter on the topic of responsibility. See page 55.
TEACHER NOTES	Consult the tables on pages 38–42 to find examples of both responsibility and failure to take responsibility in the following texts: • Consult the tables on pages 11–15 to find examples of individuals exhibiting good citizenship in the following texts: • *World History: Ancient Civilizations* • *World History: Medieval and Early Modern Times* • *Creating America: A History of the United States* • *Creating America: Beginnings through World War I* • *World History: Patterns of Interaction (survey)* • *Modern World History* • *The Americans (survey)* • *The Americans: Reconstruction to the 21st Century*

Do You Act Responsibly?

PART 1

Try this quiz to see if you behave responsibly. Circle the number that best expresses how you feel about the statement.

Agree	Sometimes Agree	Disagree	Don't Know
3	2	1	0

1. I always do what I say I will do.   3   2   1   0
2. I am on time to appointments and meetings.   3   2   1   0
3. If I make a mistake, I usually have an excuse for it.   3   2   1   0
4. I think through the consequences of my actions.   3   2   1   0
5. I think of myself as self-disciplined.   3   2   1   0
6. When I am angry, I sometimes lose control.   3   2   1   0
7. I have responsibilities to my family.   3   2   1   0
8. I have responsibilities to my friends.   3   2   1   0
9. I have responsibilities to my country.   3   2   1   0
10. I am good at following rules.   3   2   1   0

Study the statements. Which ones do you think illustrate responsible behavior? Which statements do you think concern questionable behavior? Consider how you scored on these two sets of statements. Based on your scores, do you think you qualify as a responsible person?

PART 2

Read the paragraph below and write a sentence telling what you would do.

> About two weeks ago you told a student in your class you would attend a party at that student's home. You thought your friends would be there too. Now you find out that none of them will be at the party. Instead they are going to a movie. Your friends want you to come to the movie with them. What do you do?

_____

_____

PART 3

President Harry S. Truman kept a sign on his desk that said, "The Buck Stops Here." Tell what you think that saying means and why it would be on the desk of a U.S. president.

_____

_____

Responsibility

Responsibility is a basic component of good character. Responsibility includes both accountability and obligation. A responsible person is accountable for his or her actions. This means taking credit when it is deserved and blame when it is deserved. A responsible person does not blame someone else when things go wrong. He or she recognizes that an action has caused problems for someone else.

A responsible person also recognizes obligations to self, family, community, state, and nation. Personal responsibility includes exercising self-control and taking care of one's self and family. Civic responsibilities involve obeying the law and respecting the rights of others. It also includes voting, paying taxes, and serving on juries.

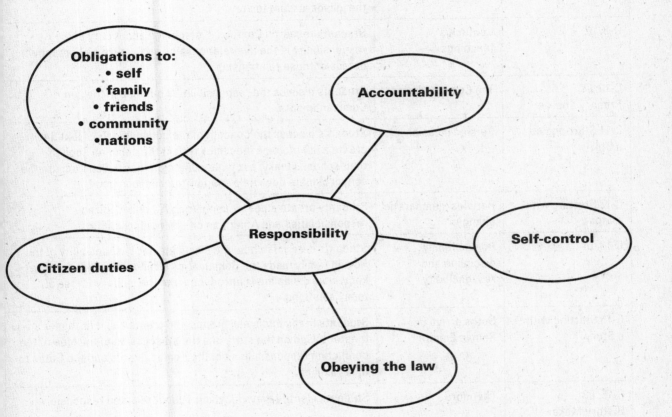

World History: Ancient Civilizations

Location	Topic	Activity
C-3, L3 Starting with a Story	Recordkeeping	Students think of school records that are kept on them. Ask how those records affect their own accountability.
C-4, L1	Hammurabi's Code	Students find a copy of Hammurabi's Code on the Internet and review laws in the code. Then they find and list examples of obligations and accountability.
C-6 Starting with a Story	Moving a village	Students stage a mock meeting of the villagers so that all points of view can be stated. Discuss what might happen if only a few of the villagers want to stay.
C-8, L2	Confucius' teachings	Students research Confucius' teachings about duty and responsibility in the five relationships and create a chart showing details of those relationships.
C-10, L1 Primary Source	Ten Commandments	Students discuss the responsibilities outlined in the Ten Commandments.
C-11 Starting with a Story	Persian invasion	Students discuss the concept of the common good. Next they create a list of items they think reflect the common good of their school. Finally, ask what obligation they have to ensure the school climate does help support the common good.
C-12 Starting with a Story	Pericles' democratic changes	Students create a poster comparing Athenian citizen responsibilities and American citizen responsibilities.
C-13, L1	Roman family discipline and responsibility	Students determine how the discipline and responsibility of the Roman family made the Roman army strong. Then ask if they know how discipline is introduced into the military forces of today's nations.
C-15 Starting with a Story	Goths arrive in Roman Empire	Students break into small groups and create a skit or reader's theater based on the story and their discussion of the idea of the conflicting responsibilities of the Roman guards and the Goths to their families.
C-15, L3 History Maker	Theodora	Students identify ways in which Theodora acted responsibly.

World History: Medieval and Early Modern Times

Location	Topic	Activity
C-2, L2	Roman political problems	Students research the percentage of eligible voters casting ballots in presidential elections over the last 25 years. Then make a line graph showing their results. Ask what happens when fewer people vote.
C-4, L1	West African families	Each student prepares a list of the obligations she/he has to the family and a list of what obligations the family has to the student. Then discuss what happens to the family if one or more members fail to fulfill the obligations.
C-6, L3 History Maker	Afonso I's letter	Students read the excerpt of Afonso's letter in the History Maker. Discuss how the letter reflects Afonso's responsibilities as leader of the Kongo people.
C-7, L1	Confucius	Students research Confucius' teachings about duty and responsibility in the five relationships and create a poster that illustrates the concepts.
C-8 Starting with a Story	Making a commitment	Students identify times in their lives either in the past or possibly in the future when they have made or might make a commitment. Then discuss the implications of failing to keep the commitment.
C-9, L1	Feudalism	Small groups of students create a poster showing the obligations and responsibilities of lords and vassals.
C-10, L1	Henry IV's repentance	Students discuss how Henry's act of repentance was a reflection of responsibility.
C-12, L1, 2	Spanish conquest in the Americas	Students write a letter to the Spanish king objecting to the treatment of conquered peoples of the Americas by Spanish conquistadors and their armies.
C-16, L2 Primary Sources	Declaration of Independence	Students read the excerpt of the Declaration of Independence in the Primary Source and identify the responsibilities that citizens have according to the document.

Creating America

A History of the United States	Beginnings through World War I	Topic	Activity
C-6, S3 One American's Story	C-6, S3 One American's Story	Minutemen	Students discuss the minutemen's pledge to defend their community. Then ask students what pledge they may have made and how that pledge signals their responsibility to act in a particular way.
C-7, S1 One American's Story	C-7, S1 One American's Story	Haym Salomon	Students make a list of people they know who have made personal sacrifices and even died for a cause in which they believe.
C-10, S1 Strange But True	C-10, S1 Strange But True	Hamilton/Burr duel	Students determine if Hamilton and Burr were responsible in their actions. Point out that anger pushed these men to this duel. Have students make a list of times when anger has pushed them to do something irresponsible.
C-10, S4 One American's Story	C-10, S4 One American's Story	Dolley Madison	Students discuss Dolley Madison's actions to save White House goods and determine if she showed responsible behavior.
C-12, S2 One American's Story	C-12, S2 One American's Story	Sequoya	Students discuss how Sequoya's actions were a responsible way to help his people. Have small groups of students research the Cherokee language and create a poster illustrating the Cherokee language.
C-14, S4 Key Players	C-14, S4 Key Players	Elizabeth Cady Stanton	Small groups of students create questions they would ask Elizabeth Cady Stanton about why she felt a responsibility to act on behalf of women and children.
C-17, S1 One American's Story	C-17, S1 One American's Story	Mother Jones	Small groups of students research the story of Mother Jones' life and create a skit based on the information they gather. The skit should focus on Mother Jones' feelings of responsibility for working people.
C-23, S1, 2 History Maker	C-23, S1, 2 History Maker	Liliuokalani/ Martí/ Muñoz	Students can role-play interviews with Liliuokalani, Martí, and Muñoz, highlighting their dedication to their people and their causes.
C-26 Literature Connection		Family responsibility	Students read the Literature Connection and identify the family responsibilities in the story.
C-29		Civil rights reformers	Students create a chart listing the reformers, the area in which they worked, and what actions they took to change the situation. When finished, students use the chart to help them write a paragraph showing how reformers took responsibility for changing conditions.
C-31, S2		Watergate scandal	Students create a list of instances in which responsible actions were not taken. Then discuss the consequences of failure to act responsibly.

World History: Patterns of Interaction

Survey	Modern World History	Topic	Activity
C-2, S1		Hammurabi's Code	Students find a copy of Hammurabi's Code on the Internet. Review laws in the code. Then find and list examples of obligations and accountability.
C-3, S4 Primary Source		Ten Commandments	Remind students that the Ten Commandments are considered the basis of law in many nations. Students determine what obligations to the community are found in this set of laws.
C-4, S4		Confucius' teachings	Students read the material under the heading "Confucius and the Social Order." Next they discuss the value of the responsibilities mandated by Confucius' teachings.
C-5, S3		Athenian democracy	Students identify the obligations an Athenian citizen had and compare them with obligations of United States citizens.
C-6, S4		Fall of Rome	Students study the chart on the Fall of the Western Roman Empire on p.174. Then have then list which causes are related to a failure of accountability or obligation either by the government or an individual.
C-13, S2		Feudalism	Students create a graphic showing the obligations of both lord and vassal in the feudalistic system.
C-17, S1 Primary Source	C-1, S2	Machiavelli	Students read the Primary Source by Machiavelli. Then have them discuss this question: "To whom does Machiavelli believe a ruler has accountability and obligations?"
C-22, S2	C-6, S2	Enlightenment ideas on government	Students list the changes in the accountability and obligations of a government after reading the material under the heading "Two Views on Government."
C-23, S2	C-7, S2	Reign of Terror	Students list the responsibilities of the Committee of Public Safety and discuss reasons why the Committee violated its obligations.
C-26, S1 Primary Source	C-10, S1	Woman suffrage	Students read the Primary Source by Emmeline Pankhurst. Then have them discuss the concept of civil disobedience.
C-31, S4	C-15, S4	Munich Conference	Students role-play a discussion between Chamberlain and Churchill after the Munich Conference about British responsibility to the people of Sudetenland and Czechoslovakia.
	C-19, S1	Democratic responsibilities	Ask students to identify the obligations individuals and government have in a democracy, using the chart Making Democracy Work on p. 1033.

The Americans

Survey	Reconstruction to the 21st Century	Topic	Activity
C-2, S4 A Personal Voice		William Penn and Native Americans	Students read the Personal Voice of William Penn and discuss how Penn's belief about accountability and obligation was different from the beliefs of other colonists.
C4, S2	C2, S1	Declaration of Independence	Remind students that the Declaration includes a long list of grievances against the king of England and calls his accountability into question. Students list ways Americans today can question accountability in government.
C-5, S2		Checks and balances	Students review the checks and balances graphic on p. 143 and determine how this system creates responsibility in government.
C-11, S1	C-4, S1	Secession of Southern states	Students role-play a discussion among members of Lincoln's cabinet about the accountability and obligations that Lincoln had to the nation.
C-15, S2	C-7, S2	Settlement houses	Students determine how reformers such as Jane Addams showed responsibility in establishing settlement houses. Then identify who offers similar services to slum areas today.
C-17, S3	C-9, S3	T. Roosevelt and health and environment	Small groups of students prepare a before-and-after poster illustrating the impact of health and environmental legislation. They should discuss how these acts demonstrate Roosevelt was acting in a responsible manner.
C-23, S1, 2	C-15, S1, 2	New Deal programs	Students review the social and economic programs of the New Deal by looking at the chart on New Deal programs on p. 706. Then students identify those programs that directly help individuals. Ask students why they think FDR felt a responsibility to aid people in the nation.
C-24, S2	C-16, S2	Munich Conference	Students role-play a discussion between Chamberlain and Churchill after the Munich Conference about British responsibility to the people of Sudetenland and Czechoslovakia.
C-29, S3 A Personal Voice	C-21, S3	Malcolm X	Students read the Personal Voice of Malcolm X. Then they discuss if they agree or disagree with his reasoning. Finally, have small groups conduct a discussion of civil disobedience.
C-32, S2	C-24, S2	Watergate scandal	Students list events in which the Nixon administration failed in its obligations to the American people. When finished, discuss the list.

Trustworthiness

Trustworthiness is a basic component of good character. Trustworthiness includes honesty, dependability, loyalty, and moral convictions. A trustworthy person tells the truth, can be depended on in all situations, and shows loyalty to family and friends. A trustworthy person has a set of moral convictions that form the basis of his or her behavior.

A trustworthy person is one that others can depend upon to keep promises and respect private information. A trustworthy person also knows, however, that keeping a confidence when the results may be harmful often is the wrong course of action. A trustworthy person can be counted on to have the courage to stand up for what she or he believes in, even if it is not a popular stand.

Trustworthiness Lesson Plan

OBJECTIVES	**1.** Define the concept of trustworthiness.
	2. Identify actions consistent with the definition of trustworthiness.
	3. Study historical examples of individuals exhibiting trustworthiness.
FOCUS AND MOTIVATE	• Have students complete the self-evaluation quiz on the handout sheet, page 45.
	• Review the questions and ask the students which three questions are about undesirable behaviors. *(3,6,7)* Discuss why they are undesirable.
INSTRUCT	**Part 1**
	• Tell students that you are investigating the character trait of trustworthiness. Ask them to come up with a definition.
	• Write the class definition on the board and compare it with a dictionary definition. *The American Heritage Student Dictionary* defines **trustworthy** as "warranting trust," and **trust** as "firm reliance on the integrity, ability, or character of a person or thing."
	• Tell the class that being a trustworthy person requires you to be reliable, to tell the truth, and to have moral convictions.
	• Use handout on page 46 to help you discuss these concepts.
	Part 2
	• Have the students silently read and react to the situation on the handout, page 45.
	• Discuss the situation and ask students to share their responses.
	• Ask which of the aspects of trustworthiness does this example deal with. *(honesty, moral convictions)*
	• Ask students to whom or what they should be trustworthy—self, family, friends, country.
	• Discuss the consequences of failing to be trustworthy to any one of the above.
	• Point out that in the course of studying history this year, they will encounter some people who were trustworthy and others who were not.

TRUSTWORTHINESS LESSON PLAN CONTINUED

Part 3

- Have the students silently read and react to the George Washington statement found on the handout, page 45.
- Discuss and clarify if necessary the concepts of honesty and trustworthiness as seen in Washington's statement.
- Then ask why they think Washington would think this was the most important of titles.
- Point out that elected leaders have a special obligation to be accountable for their behavior. Tell them that in studying history this year, they will encounter leaders and will study their behaviors to see if they were trustworthy leaders.

GROUP ACTIVITY Divide the class into small groups. Have each group put together a set of reasons explaining why a person should be trustworthy. Then the group should illustrate their list on a large sheet of paper or poster board.

WRITING ASSIGNMENT Write a composition describing a situation in which unquestioning loyalty to a friend may not be the best way to handle the situation.

FAMILY NEWSLETTER Send out the family newsletter on the topic of trustworthiness. See page 56.

TEACHER NOTES Consult the tables on pages 47–51 to find examples of individuals exhibiting trustworthiness in the following texts:

- *World History: Ancient Civilizations*
- *World History: Medieval and Early Modern Times*
- *Creating America: A History of the United States*
- *Creating America: Beginnings through World War I*
- *World History: Patterns of Interaction (survey)*
- *Modern World History*
- *The Americans (survey)*
- *The Americans: Reconstruction to the 21st Century*

Can You Be Trusted?

PART 1

Try this quiz to see how trustworthy you are. Circle the number that best expresses how you feel about the statement.

Agree	Sometimes Agree	Disagree	Don't Know
3	2	1	0

1. I always do what I say I will do.   **3   2   1   0**

2. I keep secrets and do not tell others.   **3   2   1   0**

3. If I make a mistake, I usually make an excuse for it.   **3   2   1   0**

4. I return borrowed items.   **3   2   1   0**

5. I have a set of moral convictions that I follow.   **3   2   1   0**

6. I sometimes tell "white lies."   **3   2   1   0**

7. I am loyal even if it means harm may come to someone else.   **3   2   1   0**

8. I am honest.   **3   2   1   0**

9. I have loyalties to family and friends.   **3   2   1   0**

10. I keep my promises.   **3   2   1   0**

Study the statements. Which ones do you think illustrate trustworthy behavior? Which statements do you think concern questionable behavior? Consider how you scored on these two sets of statements. Based on your scores, do you think you are trustworthy?

PART 2

Read the paragraph below and write a sentence telling what you would do.

> You have a big test coming up. Your teacher is the parent of one of your friends. The friend offers to get you the answers for the test. You really need a good grade on the test to pass the course. What do you do?

_____

_____

PART 3

President George Washington said, "I hope I shall always have firmness and virtue enough to maintain, what I consider the most enviable of all titles, the character of an honest man." Tell what you think this saying means and why Washington might think it was important.

_____

_____

Trustworthiness

Trustworthiness is a basic aspect of good character. Trustworthiness includes honesty, dependability, loyalty, and moral convictions. A trustworthy person tells the truth, can be depended on in all situations, and shows loyalty to family and friends. A trustworthy person has a set of moral convictions that form the basis of his or her behavior.

A trustworthy person is one that others can depend upon to keep promises and respect private information. A trustworthy person also knows, however, that keeping a confidence when the results may be harmful often is the wrong course of action. A trustworthy person can be counted on to have the courage to stand up for what she or he believes in, even if it is not popular.

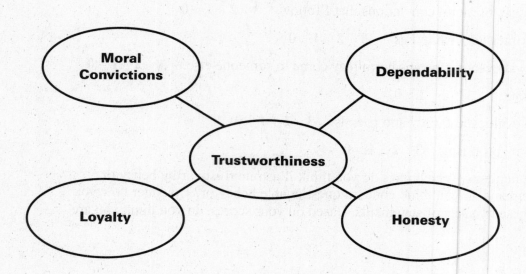

World History: Ancient Civilizations

Location	Topic	Activity
C-2, L1	Hunter-gatherers	Students discuss why trustworthiness was essential to bands of hunter-gatherers. Students make a list of times when trustworthiness of friends or family was very important.
C-3, L3	Writing system	Students discuss how a writing system such as cuneiform would affect the trustworthiness of a civilization.
C-4, Starting with a Story	Need for laws	Students identify the acts that show the builder in Starting with a Story lacked trustworthiness.
C-5, L4	Akhenaton	Students determine why the change in religious worship caused such problems. Ask student to discuss why people feel religious practices should be dependable.
C-6, L2 Primary Source	King Ezana	Students read the Primary Source and discuss how the quote illustrates a king establishing moral integrity for himself and the land. Then ask students how today's leaders or countries establish moral integrity for themselves or the country.
C-7, L2 Primary Source	Bhagavad-Gita	Students discuss how the Primary Source quote deals with trustworthiness. Then students use the Internet to find the U.S. Federal and Military oath and decide how it reflects the elements of trustworthiness.
C-8, L2	Teachings of Confucius	Students do further research into the five relationships and describe examples of each.
C-8, L3	Han bureaucracy	Students determine why trustworthiness and ethical behavior were important to the Han dynasty bureaucracy.
C-10, L1 Primary Source	Ten Commandments	Students identify which of the Ten Commandments deals with honesty.
C-11, L3	Forms of government	Students study the chart Forms of Government on p.375 and decide which form of government is most dependent on trustworthy people. Then ask students what happens to a society when leaders are not trustworthy.
C-12, L2	Use of Delian League funds	After discussing the results of Pericles' failure to be trustworthy, students role-play a scene in which leaders of other Greek city-states confront the Athenian leader.
C-13, L3 History Maker	Augustus	Students discuss if, in view of his position, Augustus' actions toward his daughter were too harsh.
C-15, Starting with a Story	Goth refugee camps	Students role-play a scene in which a Roman commander investigates Goths' claims of Roman dishonesty.

World History: Medieval and Early Modern Times

Location	Topic	Activity
C-2, L2	Roman law	Students read about Roman law under the heading "Roman Law and Government" and determine which two concepts formed the basis of the law. Then students create a poster encouraging the practice of the two concepts.
C-3, L3	Abu-Bakr	Students list the qualities that made Abu-Bakr a good choice as a leader. Ask how these qualities are related to trustworthiness.
C-4, L1	Overthrow of the Umayyads	Students read the section on the overthrow of the Umayyads. Ask if the reasons for overthrowing the Umayyads are an example of moral integrity. Students list any other reforms or changes in government that came about because people thought the government was wrong.
C-5, L1	African social life	Students determine what role a sense of loyalty played in the lives of West Africans. Then discuss loyalty to family in a modern context. Finally, write a paragraph about loyalty to your family.
C-7, L2	Scholar officials	Students list reasons why the Chinese imperial government wanted all its scholar officials to be well trained in Confucianism. Then discuss what qualities of trustworthiness would be helpful for good government workers.
C-8, L3	Bushido	Students read the information under the heading "Role of the Samurai" and decide what role trustworthiness plays in bushido. Then have students role-play an instructor and students learning aspects of a samurai's life.
C-9, L2	Chivalry	Students use a Venn diagram to compare the information on chivalry with bushido from Chapter 8, Lesson 3.
C-10 Reader's Theater	King John and the Magna Carta	Students read the Reader's Theater and then make a list of ways that King John failed to be a trustworthy leader.
C-12, L1, 2	Fall of the Aztec and Inca	Students write a paragraph explaining how disloyalty was an aspect of the fall of the Aztec and Inca empires to the Spanish.
C-13, L3	Printing press	Students make a list of the positive and negative impacts of the printing press on trustworthiness.

Creating America

A History of the United States	Beginnings through World War I	Topic	Activity
C-1, S2 Primary Source	C-1, S2 Primary Source	Iroquois Great Law	Students read the Iroquois Great Law and discuss how this agreement sets a moral code for the tribes to follow.
C-3, S1	C-3, S1	Failure of early colonies	Students read the text under the heading "Two Early Colonies Fail," p. 86. Then discuss how trustworthiness may have had an impact on these colonies.
C-7, S1,2	C-7, S1,2	Arnold and Jones	Students discuss the contrasts in the trustworthiness of Benedict Arnold and of John Paul Jones. Talk about why Arnold felt slighted. Ask students if they have ever been in a situation where they felt slighted. What was their solution?
C-7, S2	C-7, S2	Valley Forge	Students can role-play a scene from a time in the winter at Valley Forge focusing on how loyalty and trustworthiness played a role in soldiers remaining in Valley Forge even under terrible conditions.
C-12, S2	C-12, S2	Jackson's removal policy	Hold a debate on the trustworthiness of Jackson and the government policy toward Native Americans.
C-14, S3 Primary Source	C-14, S3 Primary Source	Dix Report to Massachusetts Legislature	Students review the Primary Source. Then they determine if the Dix report was accurate and trustworthy. Finally, they discuss how her reports are an example of moral uprightness.
C-17, S 3 History Maker	C-17, S 3 History Maker	Robert E. Lee	Students compare the Lee quote in America's History Makers with the one Lincoln made in Chapter 16, p. 482.
C-27, S2, 3, 4		Minorities in WWII	Students reflect on the contributions of the Tuskeegee airmen, the Navajo code talkers, and the Nisei units. Discuss why these groups would be loyal in the face of the treatment they received in the U. S.
C-28 One American's Story		LaVern Baker	Students read the LaVern Baker story in One American's Story and have a class discussion about cheating or about downloading music from the internet.
C-29		Civil rights reformers	Students create a multimedia presentation focusing on the moral uprightness of individuals featured in this chapter.
C-32, S2		Watergate	Students list the ways that Nixon and his staff were dishonest during the Watergate scandal.

World History: Patterns of Interaction

Survey	Modern World History	Topic	Activity
C-2, S4 Primary Source		Mandate of Heaven	Students discuss how the Zhou used the concept of the Mandate of Heaven to assure the conquered people that they were trustworthy. Ask why that would that be important.
C-5, S1		Concept of arete	Students read the description of *arete* found on p. 126. Then have small groups give examples of how this concept plays out in modern-day life.
C-6 Interact with History		Leadership	Students discuss the questions in Examining the Issues. Then determine how being perceived as trustworthy can influence a leaders' ability to lead.
C-9 Interact with History		Group cooperation	Students discuss the questions in Examining the Issues. Then determine the value of trustworthiness in a society that relies on cooperation to survive. Ask what might be the consequences of a failure of trust.
C-12, S1		Scholar-officials	Students identify reasons why the Chinese imperial government wanted all its scholar-officials to be well trained in Confucianism. Students list what qualities of trustworthiness would be helpful for good government workers.
C-13, S4		Role of the Church	Small groups determine why the Church became the symbol of trustworthiness during the feudal period and if that status had any disadvantages.
C-17, S1	C-1, S1	Machiavelli	Students discuss how Machiavelli's advice in *The Prince* goes counter to the elements of trustworthiness. Students write a paragraph explaining if they think ruling using Machiavelli's advice would be successful.
C-23, S3	C-7, S3	Napoleon	Students chart Napoleon's rise and his fall and identify events that led to his loss of trustworthiness.
C-28, S4	C-12, S4	Benito Juárez	Ask students to write a couple of sentences describing the impact of Juárez's reputation on Mexican history.
C-30 History through Art	C-14, S2	Propaganda	Students discuss the implications of complete Soviet control of all the media with regard to the trustworthiness of media. Then students search the Internet for articles about trustworthiness of modern-day media.
C-35, S2	C-19, S2	South African democracy	Students read about the roles of Nelson Mandela, F.W. de Klerk, and Desmond Tutu and discuss how a moral stance on a difficult issue can effect change.

The Americans

Survey	Reconstruction to the 21st Centrury	Topic	Activity
C-2, S1 One American's Story		Malinche	Small groups discuss the character of Malinche from the point of view of the Spanish and of the Indians.
C-4, S3	C-2, S2	Valley Forge	Students role-play a scene from a time in the winter at Valley Forge focusing on how loyalty and trustworthiness played a role in soldiers remaining in Valley Forge even under terrible conditions.
C-6, S1 One American's Story	C-2, S4	Washington establishes a government	Small groups of students list and discuss what issues of dependability, morality, and loyalty Washington faced.
C-7, S3	C-3, S2	Jackson's removal policy	Students hold a debate on the trustworthiness of Jackson and the government policy toward Native Americans.
C-10, S4	C-4, S1	Lincoln's character	Students write a paragraph about Lincoln's moral positions and how they affected the debate on slavery.
C-13, S2	C-5, S2	Frontier life	Students discuss how trustworthiness may have had an impact on the lives of settlers on the Plains. Ask if the plains experience can still be seen today.
C-19, S1 One American's Story	C-11, S1	Jeanette Rankin	Students draft a series of questions they would want to ask Jeanette Rankin, the only member of Congress to vote against two world wars.
C-20, S2	C-12, S2	Harding scandals	Students do research on Harding's administration and create a political cartoon reflecting one of the elements of trustworthiness.
C-25, S3	C-17, S3	Nuremberg war trials	Students discuss the trust element of moral behavior after reading about the Nuremberg war trials. Ask how these trials set a new standard of behavior for conducting war.
C-29, S1	C-21, S2	Montgomery bus boycott	Read to the students the "More About" on the Montgomery bus boycott in your Teacher's Edition. Remind students that an element of trustworthiness is dependability. Students determine how that trait was essential to the success of the boycott.
C-32, S2	C-24, S2	Watergate	Students list the ways that Nixon and his staff were dishonest in the events of the Watergate scandal. Discuss the impact of the scandal on American politics.

Family Newsletter

Character Education

This year as a part of social studies we will look at aspects of character as seen in history. For each of five character traits—citizenship, justice, respect, responsibility, and trustworthiness—we will study the elements of that trait and then look for events or individuals that involve that trait in the textbooks we use. After finding examples in history we will relate the character trait to our own lives.

Citizenship
LEARN ABOUT IT

Citizenship is one component of good character. There are many elements to citizenship. In a society we agree to live by the rule of the majority, but the majority also agrees that the minority group has rights that cannot be taken away. A good citizen agrees to respect the authority of those who are in official positions. But if those officials abuse their positions, the citizen has a right to object.

One of the most important elements of citizenship is commitment to the community. A community can be a family, a classroom, a city or town, a state, or a nation. Everyone lives with others. For a community to work well, all must cooperate and work to help one another. Sometimes these actions are called working for the common good, because everyone benefits from the work.

All citizens have both rights and responsibilities. In the United States, the U.S. Constitution and the laws of the land guarantee our rights. Our responsibilities are also outlined there.

Finally, a good citizen loves his or her country and is willing to defend the land. This is called patriotism. Patriotism is more than waving a flag and singing the national anthem. It means being loyal to the country and working hard to make sure the ideals the nation stands for are supported.

TALK ABOUT IT

Majority rules—minority rights Children often understand the idea of majority rules. However the flip side of this idea is the notion that the minority must be respected. Ask your child how respect for minority opinions can be demonstrated.

Commitment to the community Have your child think about the community in which you live. Ask what are the best aspects of this community. Then discuss ways to make the community even better than it is.

Rights and responsibilities Citizenship comes with rights but also has responsibilities. Citizens are expected to vote, serve on juries, and obey the laws. Ask your child what other civic responsibilities a citizen might have.

Patriotism Talk with your child about the principles of freedom and liberty that this nation was founded on. Help him or her to understand those ideas.

PRACTICE IT

Choose one item from the improvements to your community that you discussed in the Talk About It activity above. As a family, try to find out who might have the ability to help make that improvement happen. Then form a plan to work with that group or person.

Family Newsletter

Character Education

This year as a part of social studies we will look at aspects of character as seen in history. For each of five character traits: respect, responsibility, justice, trustworthiness, and citizenship, we will study the elements of that trait and then look for events or individuals that involve that trait in the textbooks we use. After finding examples in history we will relate the character trait to our own lives.

Justice

LEARN ABOUT IT

Justice is one basic component of good character. Justice and fairness are two sides of the same coin. When a person acts in a fair manner toward others, he or she is showing justice. When a country or a leader acts in a fair manner we call it justice. A fair or just person is open-minded. That means that the person listens to others, and studies all sides of an issue before making a judgment about it.

When practicing fairness and justice everyone is considered equal. In daily life this means you play by the rules, take turns, and share. In a just society no one has an advantage over another person.

Supporting fairness and justice also means taking action to support those ideas in your community. Fair and just leaders and countries work to make life good for everyone.

TALK ABOUT IT

Open-minded Ask your child if he or she has ever heard a rumor that turned out to be untrue. Ask what reaction they had when they found out the rumor was false. Discuss the concept of being open-minded about things they hear. Help them understand that being impartial helps promote justice by asking that all the facts be known before making a judgment.

Equality for all Read this quote from Thomas Jefferson to your child and discuss it. "It is reasonable that everyone who asks justice should do justice." Remind your child that justice and fairness extend into everyday life. Such actions as sharing, taking turns, and treating others the way they wish to be treated are examples of justice and fairness in their lives.

Play by the rules Ask your child to give you examples of situations in which individuals did not play by the rules. Then discuss how this made them feel. Next ask what they think they would do if playing by the rules means they will lose a game.

PRACTICE IT

As a family, select a cause that you think helps promote justice. Some examples may be food pantries, soup kitchens, homeless shelters, after-school tutoring, and help for the elderly or disabled. Volunteer to help an organization for a period of time. Within your family discuss the experience and how it helps to promote justice.

Family Newsletter

Character Education

This year as a part of social studies we will look at aspects of character as seen in history. For each of five character traits: respect, responsibility, justice, trustworthiness, and citizenship, we will study the elements of that trait and then look for events or individuals that involve that trait in the textbooks we use. After finding examples in history we will relate the character trait to our own lives.

Respect

LEARN ABOUT IT

Respect is one basic component of good character. Respect includes recognizing the worth and dignity of all people, self-respect, respect for the community, tolerance, and peaceful resolution of conflicts. Acting with respect allows us to live in peace and harmony in a society. A respectful person is considerate of others and makes every effort to regard each person as a valuable human being.

A respectful person understands that in every society people have disagreements. But she or he believes that those disagreements should be settled in a nonviolent manner. A respectful person is considerate of the feelings of others. A respectful person does not belittle others. A respectful person does not bully others.

TALK ABOUT IT

Worth and dignity of all people Help your child understand the concept that all humans, no matter how different they are from you, have worth. Remind them to show good manners and polite behavior toward everyone they meet.

Self-respect Respecting one's self is an important part of one's character. Ask your child what things they have done to make themselves feel proud of their actions and whether others noticed. If they did, ask what they said. If not, help your child to understand that even if the act was not recognized, it is an important part of who they are.

Respect for the community Help your child understand that we cannot live in isolation. We are a part of a larger community and we need to make that community one in which we are proud to live.

Tolerance Not every one in your child's life is like them. Ask them if they understand the idea of tolerance. Ask them to give you examples of ways they can be tolerant of others.

Peaceful resolution of conflict People living in society will have conflict. Finding a way to resolve the conflict is an important element of respect. Fighting, yelling, and ridiculing others is not a positive way to solve a problem. Ask your child to give you examples of ways to peacefully solve conflict.

PRACTICE IT

Keep a self-respect chart for a week. On the chart list an action that brought your child a sense of respect. Do the same for yourself. At the end of the week, talk about the benefits of self-respect.

Family Newsletter

Character Education

This year as a part of social studies we will look at aspects of character as seen in history. For each of five character traits: respect, responsibility, justice, trustworthiness, and citizenship, we will study the elements of that trait and then look for events or individuals that involve that trait in the textbooks we use. After finding examples in history we will relate the character trait to our own lives.

Responsibility
LEARN ABOUT IT

Responsibility is one basic component of good character. Responsibility includes practicing both accountability and obligation. A responsible person is accountable for his or her actions. This means taking the glory when it is deserved and taking blame when it is deserved. A responsible person does not pass the blame to someone else when things go wrong. He or she recognizes that an action they took caused problems or inconvenience to someone else.

A responsible person also recognizes obligations to self, family, community, state, and nation. Personal responsibility includes exercising self-control, taking care of one's self and family. Civic responsibilities involve obeying the law; respecting the rights of others; and participating in the life of the community by voting, paying taxes, and serving on juries.

TALK ABOUT IT

Accountability Discuss the idea of accountability as being expected to answer for one's actions. Ask your child what would happen in your family if no one was accountable for his or her actions. Discuss the necessity of being accountable not only to family but also to friends, and people in the community.

Obligation Tell your child that an obligation is a moral, social, legal requirement to do a certain action. Ask what obligations your child thinks a parent has. Next ask what obligations they have to you. Finally discuss obligations to others.

Personal responsibility Ask your child if they know someone who always blames others for things that go wrong. Then discuss how this behavior makes your child feel. Ask why they may think it is unfair. Continue by discussing the idea of self-control. Ask your child why self-control is an important part of good character.

Civic responsibility Have your child imagine they are in a store and see someone shoplifting. Then ask what he or she would do. Discuss their answer. Then ask what she or he would do if they saw someone hit a parked car and drive away. Discuss the answer. Mention that even though your child is a minor, she or he does participate in the life of the community and thus has a civic responsibility.

PRACTICE IT

As a family, draw up a list of responsibilities you have to each other. Be sure to have input from everyone in the household. Make a poster of the list and hang it where everyone can see it. About every two weeks, review the list to gauge how well you are holding to your responsibilities and obligations.

Family Newsletter

Character Education

This year as a part of social studies we will look at aspects of character as seen in history. For each of five character traits: respect, responsibility, justice, trustworthiness, and citizenship, we will study the elements of that trait and then look for events or individuals that involve that trait in the textbooks we use. After finding examples in history we will relate the character trait to our own lives.

Trustworthiness

LEARN ABOUT IT

Trustworthiness is a basic component of good character. Trustworthiness includes honesty, dependability or reliability, loyalty, and moral convictions. A trustworthy person tells the truth, can be depended on in all situations, and shows loyalty to family and friends. A trustworthy person has a set of moral convictions that form the basis of his or her behavior.

A trustworthy person is one that others can depend upon to keep promises and confidences. A trustworthy person also knows, however, that keeping a confidence when the results may be harmful often is the wrong course of action. A trustworthy person can be counted on to have the courage to stand up for what she or he believes in even if it is not a popular stand.

TALK ABOUT IT

Honesty Ask your child what her or she thinks this quote means, "Lying can never save us from another lie." Discuss his or her answer. You may also want to discuss the damage lies can cause to an individual's reputation and perhaps his or her future.

Dependability Have your child imagine a world in which nothing ever arrived on time—buses, television shows, dinner, etc. Ask what impact that would have on his or her life. Then ask what happens to an individual when that person fails to accomplish or meet a goal that she or he promised to do. Point out that dependability means keeping a promise and doing what you say you will do.

Loyalty Ask your child how loyalty is different from going along with the crowd. Help them understand that loyalty is being faithful to your self, your convictions, and to others.

Moral convictions Discuss with your child your moral convictions or religious beliefs. Talk about why moral convictions are an important part of good character.

PRACTICE IT

Do a family trust walk. Go outside, if possible, and pick an area to walk around in. Have the younger members of the family select an older partner. The older member closes his or her eyes and will be guided by the younger members around the space determined. The guide should bring the partner near objects in the space such as trees, tables and other objects. The guide partner listens to the "blind" partner describe what it is they are touching. Discuss the experience and how it illustrates trust.

Standards for Evaluating a Cooperative Activity

Assigned Role   recorder   reporter   materials manager   discussion leader
other _____   (circle one)

Group Cooperation	Exceptional	Acceptable	Poor
1. Helps solve conflicts to maintain agreement			
2. Shares responsibility for the activity			
3. Uses group time productively			
4. Helps the group stay on task			
5. Helps the group complete the activity			
Individual Performance			
6. Communicates ideas and concerns clearly			
7. Cooperates with other group members			
8. Fulfills assigned role			
9. Contributes ideas and effort to the group			
10. Is comfortable working with peers			
11. Demonstrates ability to motivate others			

Comments _____

_____

_____

_____

Overall rating _____

Standards for Evaluating a Group Discussion

Cooperation	Exceptional	Acceptable	Poor
1. Freely participates in discussion			
2. Listens carefully and respectfully to others			
3. Shapes personal opinions			
4. Displays tolerance for different opinions			
5. Contributes appropriate ideas and suggestions			
Individual Performance			
6. Is prepared			
7. Stays on task during discussion			
8. Communicates ideas clearly			
9. Supports own point of view with reasons or evidence			
10. Shows confidence in own judgement			
11. Demonstrates ability to modify thinking			

Comments _____

_____

_____

_____

Overall rating _____

Additional Resources

Association for Supervision and
  Curriculum Development
Character Education Network
1703 North Beauregard Street
Alexandria, VA 22311
(703) 578-9600
(800) 933-ASCD

California Department of Education
PO Box 944272
721 Capitol Mall
Sacramento, CA 95814
(916) 653-3768

California Partnership in Character
  Education
c/o Center for Youth Citizenship
9738 Lincoln Village Way
Sacramento, CA 95827
(916) 228-2322

Center for the Advancement of
  Ethics and Character
Boston University School of
Education
605 Commonwealth Avenue
Boston, MA 02215
(617) 353-3262

Center for the Fourth and Fifth R's
SUNY Cortland
PO Box 2000
Cortland, NY 13045
(607) 753-2455

Character Counts! (National Office)
4640 Admiralty Way, Suite 1001
Marina del Rey, CA 90292-6610
(310) 306-1868

Character Development Group
P.O. Box 9211
Chapel Hill, NC 27515
(919) 967-2110

Character Education Partnership
1025 Connecticut Avenue, N.W.,
Suite 1011
Washington, DC 20036
(800) 988-8081

Collaborative for Academic, Social
  and Emotional Learning (CASEL)
Department of Psychology
University of Illinois at Chicago
1007 West Harrison Street
Chicago, IL 60607
(312) 413-1012

Corporation for National and
Community Service
1201 New York Avenue, NW
Washington, DC 20525
(202) 606-5000

Education Commission of
  the States
700 Broadway, Suite 1200
Denver, CO 80203
(303) 299-3600

Ethics Resource Center
1747 Pennsylvania Avenue, NW,
Suite 400
Washington, DC 20006
(202) 737-2258

Learning in Deed
The W.K. Kellogg Foundation
One Michigan Avenue East
Battle Creek, MI 49017
(616) 969-2322

National Service-Learning
  Clearinghouse
ETR Associates
4 Carbonero Way
Scotts Valley, CA 95066
(866) 245-SERV (7378)

Pennsylvania Alliance for
  Character Education (PACE)
Pennsylvania Service-Learning
  Alliance
University of Pennsylvania
3440 Market Street, Suite 440
Philadelphia, PA 19104
(215) 573-6535

Rhode Island Department of
  Elementary and Secondary
  Education
Rhode Island Character Education
Partnership (RICEP)
255 Westminister Street
Providence, RI 02903
(401) 222-4600

RMC Research Corporation
1512 Larimer Street, Suite 540
Denver, CO 80202
(303) 825-3636
(800) 922-3636

UCLA Service Learning
  Clearinghouse
Higher Education Research Institute
Graduate School of Education
3003 Moore Hall - Box 951521
Los Angeles, CA 90095
(310) 825-1925

Utah State Office of Education
Character Education/Service-
  Learning
250 East 500 South
Salt Lake City, UT 84111
(801) 538-7606